ESSENTIAL FACTS
THE ANCIENT WORLD

Written by Fiona Macdonald
Illustrated by David McAllister

p

This is a Parragon Book
This edition published in 2001

Parragon
Queen Street House
4 Queen Street
Bath BA1 1HE, UK

ISBN 0-75256-030-1

Printed in Dubai

Produced by
Monkey Puzzle Media Ltd
Gissing's Farm
Fressingfield
Suffolk IP21 5SH
UK

Cover produced by David West Children's Books

Contents

Workmen quarrel while the tower of Babel is built in the background.

Whose palace was guarded by monsters?

King Ashurnasirpal, who ruled the Middle Eastern empire of Assyria from 883 to 859 BC, built a splendid new palace guarded by "monsters". These were Alad-lammu figures – frightening stone carvings with bulls' bodies, eagles' wings and human faces. They were meant to keep evil spirits away.

Who were the "king's ears"?

Spies who worked for the rulers of Persia were known as the "king's ears". They were introduced by King Darius I, who ruled from 522 to 486 BC. Darius divided his Persian empire into twenty provinces, and put a satrap (governor) in charge of each one. He used his spies to keep an eye – and an ear – on them!

What was the Tower of Babel?

ACCORDING TO ANCIENT HEBREW WRITERS, IT WAS THE TALLEST building on earth. It is described in a Bible story about Noah and his sons. They wanted to build a tower all the way up to heaven. But God did not want the tower, and turned all the workmen's words into nonsense sounds. They could not understand each other, so the tower was never completed. Historians think this story may have been based on real buildings, called ziggurats, built in Babylon from around 900 BC.

When was writing invented?

Writing was invented around 3500 BC, in Sumer (part of present-day Iraq). The Sumerians were rich, and needed to keep records of their goods and money. They used pens made from reeds to make scratch-marks on "tablets" of soft, damp clay. These tablets were dried in the sun to preserve them.

What were found in the "death-pits"?

Bodies and treasures! Archaeologists have discovered over 1,500 tombs at the Sumerian city of Ur. Most date from around 2500 BC. These "death-pits" contained jewellery, head-dresses, statues, musical instruments, furniture – and the bodies of servants, buried with their royal masters so they could care for them in the next world.

Why did people start farming?

Who gave his name to new laws?

Hammurabi, king of Babylon from 1792 to 1750 BC, conquered new lands and created a powerful empire. To encourage its peoples to live peacefully together, he drew up a set of strict laws called the Code of Hammurabi. These laws governed everything from family life and adoption, to farming and trade.

Where were shellfish worth more than gold?

A shellfish called "murex" was treasured throughout ancient Greece, Rome and the Middle East, where it was used to make a deep-purple dye. This was so expensive that only kings and queens could afford to wear purple clothes.

PEOPLE FIRST STARTED FARMING IN THE MIDDLE EAST, AROUND 10,000 YEARS ago. Faced with a changing climate and a water shortage, they could no longer survive as nomads moving from place to place. They had to settle down near reliable water-supplies. Living in one village, all year round, they noticed that seeds of wild grain began to sprout where they had fallen on the ground. So they scattered more seeds, watched them grow, and harvested the ripe grain.

Who invented "murex" dye?

The dye was invented by the Phoenicians – sailors and traders who lived on the eastern shores of the Mediterranean Sea in the first millennium BC. Dyeing cloth was a long, messy and smelly process. Some 10,000 shellfish were needed to make the dye for one long robe.

Merchants haggle over the price of a shipment of "murex" dye at a quayside in Phoenicia.

Many Egyptians still farm as they did 3,000 years ago, using a shaduf (top left-hand of picture) to transport water from the river to irrigate the land.

Who paid their taxes by doing hard labour?

Most Egyptian men worked as farmers. Sometimes, the government demanded a share of their harvest as tax. But more often they were ordered to work as labourers on government building-projects, such as pyramids, temples and tombs. The ancient Egyptians had no big machines to help them build, so they used thousands of these labourers instead. If farmers refused to work, they might be beaten and have their houses and tools taken away.

Who was glad when their fields were flooded?

Egyptian farmers! They cultivated land beside the River Nile, and each year – between June and September – the river waters flooded their fields. When the floods went away, they left behind a layer of sticky, black mud. The mud was rich and fertile, and ideal for growing wheat, barley and vegetables.

What did boats and books have in common?

Both were made from tall reeds that grew beside the River Nile, called papyrus. Bundles of papyrus were tied together to make boats. Thin strips of it were dampened, laid on top of each other, then pressed together to make a form of paper. Papyrus sheets were sewn together to make scrolls, which the Egyptians read like books.

Were there dangers down by the river?

Yes! Crocodiles lurked in the shallow reed-beds, and hippos lay hidden under the water. Both have very sharp teeth. Mummified bodies surviving from ancient Egypt show that many people lost limbs – or were killed – by animal attacks.

What caused terrible toothache?

Egyptian people often suffered from painful broken teeth and gum infections, caused by eating bread! Egyptian bread was nourishing and tasty, but it contained sharp grains of sand, blown in from the desert, and tiny fragments of grit from the stones used by women to grind wheat and barley into flour.

Where was the Red Land?

Deshret, which means the Red Land, was the ancient Egyptians' name for the hot, dry desert that made up most of their country. No one could live comfortably in the desert, and the Egyptians considered it a place of death. So, almost all Egyptian people lived on a narrow strip of land beside the River Nile. The Egyptians called this Kemet, the Black Land. They believed that black was a lucky colour – a sign of new life and hope.

Why did people put beds on the roof ?

It was a way of keeping cool in the hot Egyptian climate. Many Egyptian houses had flat roofs, which people used as extra rooms for sleeping or doing work like weaving. It was quite safe to leave your bed and weaving looms on the roof, because for most of the year it hardly ever rained.

Which household pets guarded grain stores?

Cats! The Egyptians were probably the first people to tame cats. They encouraged wild cats to live on their farms, to kill the rats and mice that ate stores of grain. Later, Egyptians kept cats as pets in their homes. Can you guess the Egyptian word for cat? It was "miw"!

Egyptian homes often had only one storey, with steps going up to the roof. They were usually made from mud-brick.

A foreman explains the plans, as the pyramids at Giza are built behind him.

Why were pharaohs buried in pyramids?
Pyramids were thought of as stairways, linking earth to heaven. The Egyptians believed that a pyramid's pointed shape would help a dead pharaoh's spirit climb up into the sky, to join the gods living there.

How did a pyramid guard a pharaoh's body?
Within most pyramids, there were secret doors, traps and hidden passages designed to confuse tomb-robbers.

Which is the biggest pyramid?
The biggest is the Great Pyramid at Giza, in northern Egypt. It is over 147 m (482 ft) high, and is breathtaking to see. The Great Pyramid was built to house the tomb of Khufu, or Cheops, who was pharaoh around 2500 BC. Three smaller pyramids containing the tombs of his wives stand nearby.

Why did a queen wear a beard?

QUEEN HATSHEPSUT WAS THE WIFE OF THE PHARAOH THUTMOSE II. WHEN he died around 1479 BC, his son and heir was still a young boy. So, Hatshepsut had herself crowned pharaoh in his place, even though women did not normally rule. She ordered a splendid temple to be built, containing many sculptures of her. They show her wearing a false beard, and carrying a crook and a flail. All three were signs of kingship.

What happened if you touched a pharaoh?

You might get hurt, or even killed. The Egyptians believed that the pharaoh was more than a man. His body also contained the spirit of the god Horus, and this gave him terrifying power. So, everyone treated the pharaoh with great respect.

Why did pharaohs wear a double crown?

It showed that the pharaoh was king of all Egypt. At first, Egypt was divided into two separate kingdoms – Upper Egypt and Lower Egypt. After 3100 BC, the two kingdoms were united. So, the pharaoh wore a double crown, called a pschent, with a white top (for Upper Egypt) and a red bottom (for Lower Egypt).

Did pharaohs lead soldiers into battle?

Yes, the pharaoh was army commander, head of government and chief priest! Many paintings and carvings show pharaohs in chariots, riding off to war. Egyptian armies invaded Libya, Nubia (present-day Sudan), Syria and the Hittite kingdoms (in modern Turkey).

What was life like at the "great house"?

LIFE WAS VERY GRAND AND LUXURIOUS – AND ALSO VERY BUSY – AT THE "GREAT house" or per–aa. This was the Egyptian word for the royal palace, and it is where the word "pharaoh" comes from. The pharaohs were the rulers of Egypt. They lived in the royal palaces, which were vast complexes of public and private rooms. Hundreds of people worked there, including priests, government officials, scribes, army commanders, servants and slaves.

A pharaoh and his queen surrounded by their officials and scribes.

How long did it take to make a mummy?

The head of the mummy of Yuya – the father of an Egyptian Queen called Tiye.

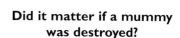

It took about seventy days to make a corpse

into a mummy. Embalmers pulled the brain out through the nose. They removed the lungs, liver, stomach and intestines, and stored them in containers called canopic jars. Then, they packed the body with natron – a type of salt which removed all moisture and stopped the body rotting. The corpse was rubbed with oils and spices, and wrapped in bandages. Finally, it was placed in a coffin, and buried in a tomb.

What did tomb-paintings show?

The Egyptians believed the "afterlife" would be very much like the life they enjoyed on earth. So they decorated their tombs with wall-paintings showing themselves and their loved ones busy with everyday activities, such as working in the fields, fishing, or relaxing with friends.

Why was a village built near the Valley of the Kings?

A village called Deir el-Medina was built around 1550 BC, to house the families of workers building royal tombs in the nearby Valley of the Kings – a famous burial ground for pharaohs. The village survived for about 500 years.

The workers' village of Deir el Medina, with the Valley of the Kings in the background.

Did it matter if a mummy was destroyed?

Yes, it was a disaster! The Egyptians believed that a dead person's spirit would only survive for as long as the body was preserved. The spirit would fade away even if the mummy was just damaged. So, embalmers took great care to make sure that a mummy was complete.

Which was more precious, silver or gold?

Silver was much more valuable than gold. There were many rocks containing gold in the Egyptian desert, but silver had to be brought from distant lands. This made it expensive. The Egyptians believed silver was the bones of gods and goddesses, and gold was their flesh.

What were shabtis for?

Shabtis were little model figures of men and women. The Egyptians believed the dead would be asked to work hard in the afterlife – but that shabtis could work on their behalf. The richest people paid for 365 shabtis to be put in their tombs – one for each day of the year!

The Egyptians believed in life after death. So, they filled their tombs with favourite treasures, useful objects, clothes, food and drink, so they could enjoy them in the afterlife. Treasure showed a dead person's rank, and made sure that his or her spirit would be treated with respect.

The mummy of Pharaoh Mernephtah (1236 - 23 BC).

How long did Tutankhamun lie undisturbed?

TUTANKHAMUN'S MUMMY REMAINED SAFE FOR AROUND 3,249 YEARS! HE was only about nineteen when he died around 1327 BC, and was probably buried the same year. His burial chamber lay safe until AD 1922, although the outer sections of his tomb were disturbed by robbers. Tutankhamun was pharaoh at a time when Egypt was very rich and its craftsmen very skilled, so his tomb contained some of the most magnificent treasures of ancient Egypt.

A pharaoh's tomb is prepared for him. His mummy case is surrounded by shabtis.

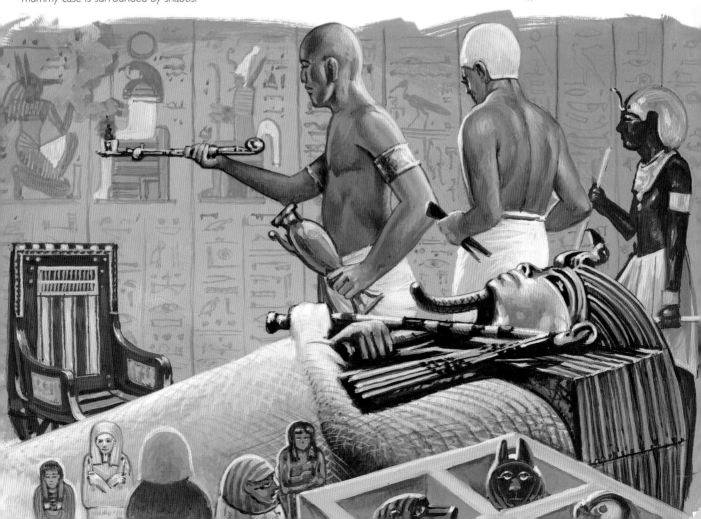

Could anyone enter a temple?
No! Temples were homes for the gods. Only priests, priestesses and the pharaoh dared set foot there. Once inside a temple, they performed rituals to help the whole community – dancing, singing, and placing offerings of food and drink in front of statues of the gods.

How did ordinary Egyptians worship the gods?
Ordinary people worshipped in two different ways. Firstly, they said prayers and made offerings at little shrines (holy places) in their homes. Secondly, they took part in great processions, escorting statues of the gods from one temple to another on festival days.

Which pharaoh invented a new religion?

PHARAOHS TRADITIONALLY HONOURED AMUN, THE CREATOR-GOD. BUT Amenhotep IV, who was pharaoh from 1352 to 1336 BC, worshipped the sun-god Aten. He changed his own name to Akhenaten ("glory of the sun-god") and built a city full of temples honouring his god. He also ordered the names of all other gods to be chipped off temple walls. But after Akhenaten died, people went back to worshipping the old gods, and his new city was abandoned.

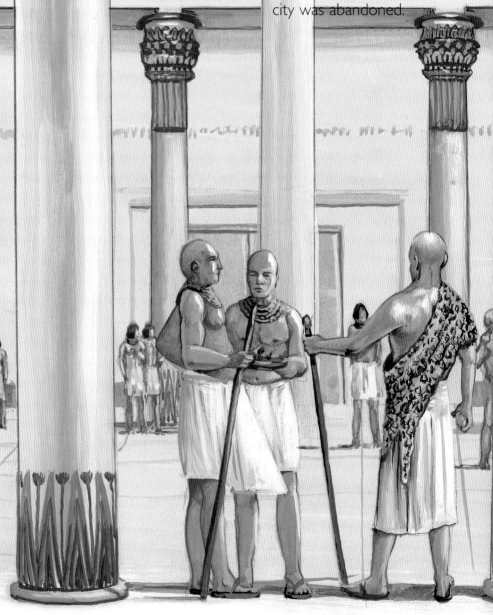

After the Pharaoh and the nobles and senior officials, Egyptian priests were the most important people in society. They ran the temples, where the gods were believed to live.

Who wrote books of magic spells?

Trained professional writers, called scribes, copied out all kinds of religious documents, as well as stories, poems and government records. They also wrote out books of magic spells, which were buried alongside mummies to guide their spirits in the afterlife.

Which god ruled the underworld?

The mighty god Osiris, lord of the dead, ruled the underworld where dead spirits lived for ever. Myths told how Osiris was killed by his brother, Seth, and cut into pieces. He was put back together again by the jackal-headed Anubis, god of mummies and mummy-makers.

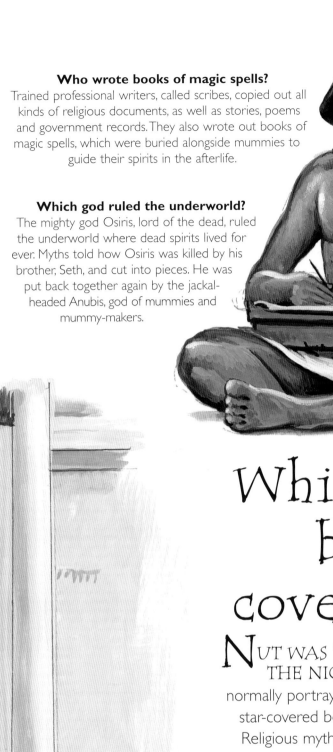

This scribe has a papyrus on his lap and he is writing with a brush made from reed.

Which goddess's body was covered in stars?

NUT WAS THE BEAUTIFUL GODDESS OF THE NIGHT SKY. EGYPTIAN ARTISTS normally portrayed her as a tall, slender woman, arching her star-covered body protectively over the earth far below. Religious myths told how Nut swallowed the sun every evening, then gave birth to it again each morning. Egyptians prayed to Nut as a kindly mother, asking her to give them new life in the world of the dead.

Who was "he who is far above"?

This was Horus, the hawk-headed god of the sky. His bright eyes represented the sun and moon. Like him, they seemed to fly far above the earth. Horus was the protector of pharaohs, and statues of him stood in many royal tombs to guard the pharaoh's spirits.

Who was the most powerful god?

The Egyptians worshipped over 2,000 gods and goddesses. Amun, creator of the world, was the most powerful. In many statues and carvings, he is shown as part human, part ram.

Who took ten years to travel home?

After the Trojan war ended, the Greek warrior Odysseus set sail for his home on the island of Ithaca. But he met so many dangers and had so many adventures that his journey took ten years. The story of Odysseus was first written down by the Greek poet Homer.

Which city had walls built by giants?

Mycenae – a powerful city that controlled southern Greece from around 1600 to 1200 BC – was surrounded by massive stone walls, and guarded by a gateway decorated with lions. Visitors to Mycenae said the walls were so big they could only have been built by giants.

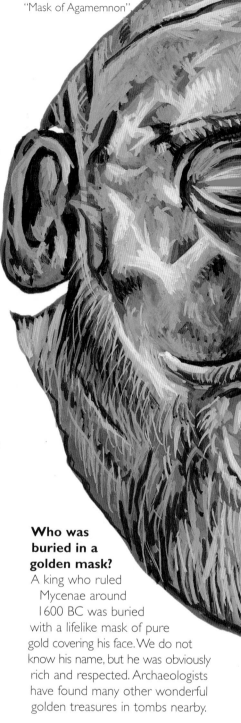

This gold mask is called the "Mask of Agamemnon".

Who killed a monster in a maze?

ACCORDING TO LEGEND, THE GREEK HERO THESEUS KILLED A TERRIBLE monster that lurked deep inside a maze in a royal palace on Crete. This monster, half-man, half-bull, was called the Minotaur, and ate children sent as tribute to Minos, king of Crete. Historians think the story of the Minotaur and the maze may have grown up because King Minos's palace had over 1,000 rooms. It was so big that all visitors got lost inside it!

Theseus killed the Minotaur after chasing it into its labyrinth.

Who was buried in a golden mask?

A king who ruled Mycenae around 1600 BC was buried with a lifelike mask of pure gold covering his face. We do not know his name, but he was obviously rich and respected. Archaeologists have found many other wonderful golden treasures in tombs nearby.

Which fruit was the gift of a goddess?

Myths tell how the first olive tree was planted by the goddess Athene, in the city of Athens. The Athenians ate olives with bread and cheese, or crushed them to make oil for cooking and cleaning. They were so grateful to Athene, they made her their own special goddess.

From around 2200 to 1450 BC, kings on the island of Crete controlled shipping and trade throughout the Mediterranean. They built huge palaces, decorated with wall-paintings and statues. These show scenes of people worshipping bulls, and goddesses with snakes.

Why did the Greeks build a wooden horse?

DURING THE TROJAN WAR, THE GREEKS SURROUNDED THE

city of Troy. They camped outside its walls for ten years, but could not break through. So, they built a huge, hollow horse out of wood, hid some soldiers inside it, and pretended to sail away. Full of curiosity, the Trojans pulled the horse into their city. At night, the Greek soldiers crept out of the horse and opened the gates to let in the rest of their army. Troy was captured and destroyed.

Greek soldiers prepare to capture the city of Troy.

Which war started when a wife left her husband?

Poets tell how Helen, the beautiful wife of the Greek king Menelaus, was lured away by Paris, the son of the king of Troy. To win Helen back, the Greeks attacked Troy. This started the legendary Trojan War, which may have been fought around 1100 BC.

15

Where did the people have power?

The people had power in cities like Athens, which had democratic governments. All adult men who lived there had the right to vote for government officials, and to help make laws. However, this right did not extend to women, foreigners and slaves.

Athenian men debate and argue about politics and government. In the background is the Acropolis.

Who ran the first marathon, and why?

ACCORDING TO MYTH, THE FIRST MARATHON WAS RUN BY a Greek messenger called Pheidippides. After the Battle of Marathon in 490 BC, he ran all the way to Athens to bring the good news that the Greeks had defeated the Persians. But the distance was so far – about 42 km (26 mi) – that he collapsed and died. The distance of the modern marathon run at the Olympic Games is supposed to be the same as that covered by Pheidippides.

Who were the Greeks' bitter enemies?

The Greeks fought bitterly with the Persians, who ruled an empire stretching from Turkey to India. Led by the kings Darius and Xerxes, Persian armies invaded Greece in 490 BC and 480 BC. After mighty battles at Marathon, Plataea and Salamis, the Persians were defeated.

Where did Greek women spend their days?

Mostly at home! Young girls and respectable married women did not go out of doors without a man or some slaves to escort them, unless there was a festival. Instead, they stayed in the women's rooms of their home, cooking, bringing up children, spinning and weaving.

Who threw wine at the walls?

After they had eaten and drunk a lot of wine, the guests at a Greek dinner-party played a game called kottabos. They held their wine-cups by one handle, spun them round, and flicked the last drops of wine at a target on the wall.

Why did the Greeks leave home?

The Greek population was increasing, and there was not enough land to grow food. To escape poverty and hunger, Greek families left to settle in new colonies around the Mediterranean Sea. In this way, Greek civilization spread to many lands outside Greece.

Men relax at a dinner party while women sing and dance to entertain them.

Who slept on beds of rose petals?

According to Greek historians, life in the new Greek colonies was so comfortable that settlers slept on rose-petal beds. This was not true, but colonies such as Syracuse on the island of Sicily did become very rich. People who lived there could afford many luxuries.

Why were ships so important?

SEA TRAVEL WAS THE EASIEST WAY TO REACH MANY PLACES IN

Greece. The Greek mainland was rocky and mountainous, and there were few roads. Greeks also made their homes on hundreds of other islands, widely scattered across the sea. Ferries and cargo ships had to carry people and goods from port to port around the coast. Ships were also important in war. Greek fighters rowed huge warships called triremes to drive away invaders.

Which city trained the best soldiers?

Soldiers from the city of Sparta were said to be the bravest and best in all Greece. Spartan boys were taken away from their families when they were about eight years old, to learn how to fight and endure pain. They spent the next 25 years with the army!

Spartan soldiers were feared throughout Greece.

Where did plays win prizes?
In many cities in ancient Greece,
there were festivals in which actors
recited the verse and performed
the songs and dances of new
plays. The writers of the best plays
were rewarded with "crowns"
of laurel leaves, and
sometimes also with rich
prizes.

Greek actors wore
masks showing tragic
or comic faces.

Who created fabulous works of art?

Greek potters, sculptors, stonemasons, jewellers and weavers were famous
for their arts. They were highly skilled, and made statues and buildings to
adorn cities, clothes and jewels for people to wear, and pottery for
ornaments or serving food.

Was it rude to swear the Hippocratic Oath?

No! According to legend, the Hippocratic Oath was a solemn promise made
by Greek doctors. It was named after Hippocrates (c.460–370 BC), the
"father of medicine" who taught students to observe patients scientifically,
and to do their best to help sick people at all times.

What happened on Mount Olympus?

FEASTING, FIGHTING AND FALLING IN LOVE! GREECE'S HIGHEST PEAK,

Mount Olympus, was believed to be home to the Greek
gods and goddesses. They enjoyed the same pleasures and
suffered the same problems as ordinary men and women –
but on a much grander scale! Zeus, king of the gods, sent
thunder and lightning. His jealous wife, Hera, protected
married women. Other gods included Athene, goddess of
learning; Aphrodite, goddess of love; and Apollo, god of music.

Why did Archimedes jump out of his bath?

Because he had worked out the answer to an important engineering problem – why things float in water. He was so excited that he jumped up, shouting *"Eureka!"* ("I've got it!"). Archimedes lived around 250 BC, and made many scientific discoveries that are still used today.

Who was killed for asking questions?

The philosopher Socrates (469–399 BC) taught his students to ask questions. This made him unpopular with the city council in Athens, who feared he would teach everyone to question the way the city was run. They put Socrates in prison, and made him drink poison.

Why were cows covered with flowers?

To please the gods! On holy days, the Greeks killed animals as sacrifices. They hoped that the gods would be kind to them in return. Animals for sacrifice were washed, brushed, and decorated with flowers. They were led to temples, and put to death by priests.

Who ran races to honour the gods?

ATHLETES WHO TOOK PART IN SPORTS FESTIVALS, KNOWN AS "GAMES", ran to honour the gods. There were many different games in Greece. The Olympic Games were probably the oldest, and most famous. They began in 776 BC, in honour of Zeus, and were held every four years. Athletes ran, wrestled, boxed and raced chariots. Only men could take part – although there were special women-only games in non-Olympic years.

Competitors who won the Olympic Games became very famous and were treated as celebrities in their hometowns.

A Roman senator is taken to the senate in a litter carried by slaves.

Which provincial people were the victims of a volcano?

In AD 79, the volcano Vesuvius in southern Italy erupted, belching out clouds of steam, red-hot cinders and poison gas, and pouring out streams of lava. The citizens of Pompeii, a rich, seaside town, were trapped in their homes. Most were killed, and Pompeii was buried.

What might you find under Rome's city streets?

DRAINS AND SEWERS! THE ROMANS WERE GREAT engineers. They designed complicated systems to bring fresh water for drinking and washing to the city of Rome, and to carry away dirty water and other waste hygienically. The richest homes had running water, carried in lead pipes, while ordinary people got fresh water from public drinking-fountains. The largest sewer, called the cloaca maxima, was so big that a horse and cart could drive through it.

How did a wolf help to create Rome?

According to legend, Rome was founded by a warrior called Romulus. He and his brother Remus were parted from their mother when they were babies, and nearly died. They were saved by a she-wolf, who nursed and protected them. When he had grown up, Romulus built Rome and named it after himself.

Where are the Seven Hills?

Rome was built on the Seven Hills. Archaeologists think the city began as a few scattered villages built on two of these hills. Around 750 BC, the villages joined together and the city began to spread over the neighbouring hills. By AD 300, over a million people lived there.

Who made new laws?

Retired government officials, called senators, helped to make the laws before 27 BC, when Rome was still a republic (a country where people vote for their leaders). But after this date, Rome was ruled by emperors – men who had absolute power to make their own laws.

Pompeii was buried under tonnes of hot ash.

Where were the world's first high-rise flats built?

They were built in Ostia, a busy port close to Rome.

By around AD 300, Ostia was home to almost 100,000 people – mostly sailors, traders and labourers, and the shopkeepers and craftsmen who provided their supplies. Blocks of flats known as *insulae* (islands) were built to house these workers and their families. They were crowded, noisy, dirty and cold. The flats often burnt down, because people used little coal-braziers to heat their rooms.

Did all roads lead to Rome?

Yes, all the biggest ones did. The Romans built about 85,000 km (53,000 m) of roads across their empire, designed to link distant provinces with Rome. The roads were used by the army and by traders coming to Rome to sell goods and food.

The Romans invented aqueducts that carried water across the countryside to the cities of the Empire.

Who worked hard on country estates?

Slaves! Wealthy Roman families liked to spend time away from the noise and bustle of Rome. So they purchased country estates, with a fine "villa", or house, surrounded by fields and farms. All the hard work on these estates was done by slaves.

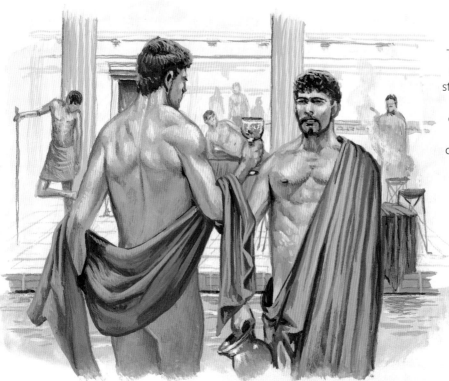

What were the Blues and Greens?

They were rival teams of chariot-drivers. Chariot-racing, at a huge stadium called the Circus Maximus, was one of the most popular entertainments in Rome. Drivers raced in light, two-wheeled chariots pulled by horses. Crowds cheered on the Reds, Whites, Blues or Greens.

Roman men often had business meetings at the baths.

Why did Romans spend so long in the bath?

BECAUSE IT WAS FUN! MOST ROMAN CITIES HAD HUGE PUBLIC

baths. They were a favourite place to relax and meet friends. Visitors to the baths got clean by rubbing themselves all over with olive oil, or by sweating in clouds of steam. They could enjoy a swim in pools of warm water, have a massage, read, eat a snack, or take part in sports. The Romans believed, quite rightly, that keeping clean helped to keep them healthy.

How many spectators did the Colosseum hold?

The Colosseum was the biggest arena in Rome, and it held about 50,000 people. It was made mostly of concrete, a Roman invention. It had a movable canvas roof, to shade spectators from the sun, and the floor was covered with sand – to soak up all the blood.

Why did priests cut animals open?

They did this to predict the future. After an animal had been sacrificed to the gods, a priest called a haruspex would examine the dead beast's liver. If it was misshapen or diseased, that meant the gods were angry and something terrible was about to happen

Who met to say prayers in holes underground?

Until AD 313, Christianity was banned throughout the Roman Empire. So, the first Christians in Rome had to meet in secret. They used deep underground passages (called catacombs) to bury their dead, and to say secret prayers.

When did Roman girls sigh?

WHEN THEY SAW THE TOP GLADIATORS, WHO ENTERTAINED CROWDS IN huge arenas like the Colosseum. Gladiators were as popular as rock stars today, and were famous for having many girlfriends. Their strength and fitness made them attractive, and the fact that most were doomed to die gave them extra glamour. Most gladiators were prisoners captured in war, or criminals. Many were specially trained in gladiator schools. They fought with each other, or against wild animals brought from Africa.

Who made offerings every day?
Roman housewives, their husbands and children left food and drink, or burned incense, in front of a little shrine in their living room. It contained statues of ancient spirits called the "lares and penates", who looked after each household and all its goods.

Which gods guarded the city?
The Romans worshipped many gods. Jupiter, the king of the gods, protected Roman lands. Janus (who had two faces, looking forwards and backwards) watched over the city gates. Vesta was the goddess of Roman homes. Her priestesses tended a holy flame. If it went out, it was believed Rome's power would collapse.

Roman emperors loved to watch gladiatorial fights. They especially enjoyed watching Christians being fed to the lions.

How far did soldiers march each day?

Up to 30 km (18.5 m)! They marched from army camps and forts to places where they were needed for fighting. Where possible, they travelled along straight, well-made roads. To help them march, they wore special caligae (army boots) with thick, hob-nailed soles.

Legionary soldiers had to carry their belongings with them, wherever they marched.

How big was the Roman Empire?

AT ITS LARGEST, IN THE SECOND CENTURY AD, THE ROMAN EMPIRE stretched from Scotland and Germany in the north and west, to Egypt and Turkey in the south and east. The Romans introduced their customs, ideas and beliefs to the lands they ruled. Throughout the Empire, all the conquered peoples had to pay the same taxes and obey the same laws as those in Rome. Government officials all had to speak Latin, the language of the Romans.

Who were Marius's mules?

This name was given to Roman foot-soldiers. After the Roman army was reorganized by General Marius (c.157–86 BC), each soldier had to carry a heavy pack on his back – like a mule! The pack contained weapons, armour, tools for building a camp, cooking pots, dried food and spare clothes.

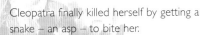

Cleopatra finally killed herself by getting a snake – an asp – to bite her.

Which Roman general gave up power for love?

MARCUS ANTONIUS (83–30 BC), A BRILLIANT ARMY commander who led Roman troops in France and North Africa, was also a top politician in Rome. But he fell in love with Cleopatra, Queen of Egypt. This led to Rome fighting a war against Antonius and Cleopatra, who were defeated at the Battle of Actium in 31 BC. Antonius later committed suicide after receiving a false report of Cleopatra's death.

Why was Trajan's Column carved?

It was carved to commemorate the Roman conquest of Dacia (Romania) in AD 106. Trajan (ruled AD 98–117) was a famous soldier who became emperor. The column is a stone pillar standing in the "forum", or market square, in Rome. It is decorated with carvings of 2,500 Roman soldiers winning wars.

Who built walls to guard the frontier?

The emperors Hadrian (ruled AD 117–138) and Antoninus Pius (ruled AD 138–161) ordered walls to be built in northern Britain, to defend the Roman Empire from attack by native tribes. These became Hadrian's Wall, and the Antonine Wall.

Who signed up for 20 years?

Male citizens of Rome who volunteered for the army signed up for this long. A soldier received excellent training and was well-paid, but had to buy food, clothes and weapons out of his wages. When he retired, he was given money or land, to help start a business or a farm.

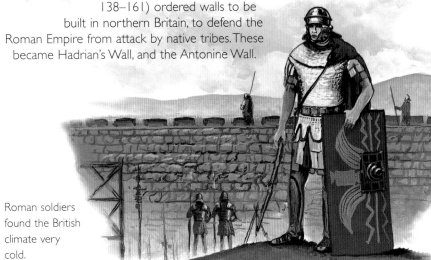

Roman soldiers found the British climate very cold.

Where could you meet head-hunters, druids and bards?

YOU COULD MEET THEM ALL IN A CELTIC VILLAGE. CELTIC CIVILIZATION SPREAD across Europe around 750 BC. The Celts were farmers and metalworkers. They saved the skulls of important enemies, so that they could share their spirits' power. They had priests called druids, and enjoyed listening to poets, called bards, singing songs about heroic deeds. Celtic power crumbled after the Roman general Julius Caesar conquered Gaul (France, Belgium, the Netherlands and southern Germany) between 58 and 51 BC.

Which queens led armies against Rome?
Queen Boudicca (died AD 62) led her Celts against Roman armies in England. Her soldiers attacked London, and left it in ruins. Queen Zenobia (died AD 274) fought against the Romans in Syria, but was captured and paraded in chains through the streets of Rome.

Where was the "evil empire"?
This was what the Romans called Persia (present-day Iran). In AD 224, a warlike family of kings called the Sassanids seized power there. Roman emperor Valerian (ruled AD 253–260) led his armies against the Sassanids, but they killed him

Who rushed into battle with no clothes on?
Celtic warriors believed that fighting naked gave them magic power. The Celts thought it was better to die fighting bravely in battle, than live and face defeat – for a brave warrior's spirit would soon be reborn.

The Celts were very ferocious enemies!

Which warlike tribes helped to name modern Europe?

From around AD 400, Germanic peoples such as the Angles, Saxons and Franks replaced the old Roman Empire with new kingdoms. They gave their names to conquered lands. The Angles and Saxons settled in "Angle-land", or England, and the Franks conquered France.

The Saxons resisted Roman rule and created their own kingdoms.

Why did the Roman Empire collapse?

The Empire had grown too large to defend, and many Roman emperors did not rule well. Some were mad, weak or foolish, others were corrupt. They could not cope with economic problems, citizens' riots, religious quarrels and civil wars. The last emperor fled from Rome in AD 476.

What was the Byzantine Empire?

In AD 330, Emperor Constantine (c. AD 274–337) moved the capital of the Empire east from Rome to the city of Byzantium (in modern-day Turkey). He renamed it Constantinople. The western half of the Empire, around Rome, declined. But the eastern half became the powerful Byzantine Empire, which maintained Roman traditions for centuries.

Which famous horsemen threatened Rome?

L ED BY ATTILA (C. AD 406–453), HORDES OF INVADERS CALLED HUNS REACHED Italy and threatened to destroy Rome. They came from central Asia, where they lived as nomads keeping horses, sheep and goats. The Huns were famous for their riding skills. It was said that they could sleep while they rode – so they advanced twice as fast as other armies. In battle, they could turn right round in the saddle, and shoot backwards at their enemies while riding quickly away.

What were "were-jaguars"?

These were strange, frightening creatures – half human baby, half snarling jaguar. They are portrayed in carvings and sculptures created by the Olmec people who lived in Central America from 1200 to 400 BC. They were probably meant to link humans to the spirits of the wild animals around them.

Where were ball-courts built?

BALL-COURTS – WALLED, OPEN SPACES, SURROUNDED BY SEATS – WERE built throughout Central America and the Caribbean. They were used for a ball-game which was part sport, part religious ritual. Players tried to hit a rubber ball through hoops high above ground without using their hands or feet.

Where can you see the Great Serpent?

The Great Serpent Mound is in the present-day state of Ohio, USA. It is a huge, raised bank of earth, 400 m (1,312ft) long, shaped like a snake swallowing an egg. It was built around AD 200, probably for religious reasons.

Who invented picture-writing, and studied the stars?

The Maya people of Central America, whose civilization thrived from AD 250 to 900, were the only early Americans with a complete writing system. It used picture symbols to show sounds, ideas and numbers. They were also expert astronomers, with a complicated calendar based on planets and stars.

Where were pueblos found?

Villages called pueblos were built in the south-west of North America. Each pueblo was made of hundreds of rooms, joined together. They had underground chambers, called "kivas", used for religious ceremonies. Many had ball-courts, too.

The losing team in the ball-game might be sacrificed to the gods.

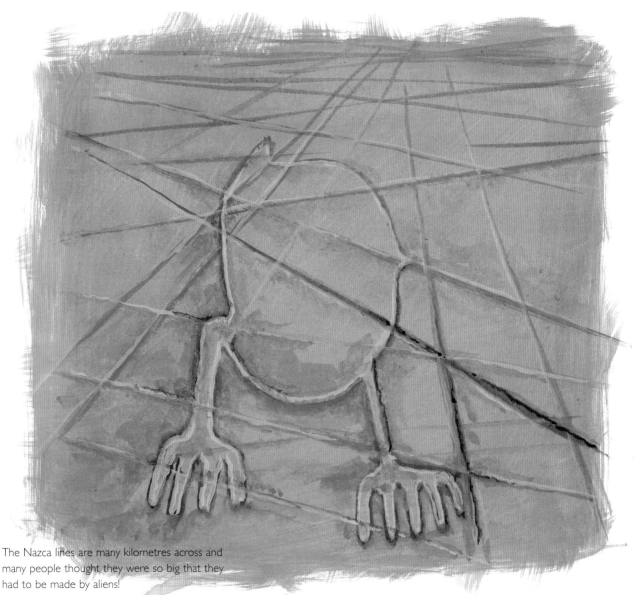

The Nazca lines are many kilometres across and many people thought they were so big that they had to be made by aliens!

Why was a spider drawn in the desert?

A spider is one of many huge shapes, including birds, monkeys and whales, created by the Nazca people who lived in southern Peru from AD 200 to 700. Possibly, the shapes are pictures of constellations, or signs pointing to a holy site in the mountains.

Why were the "three sisters" so important?

They kept early American farmers alive! The "three sisters" were the most important food-crops: maize, beans and squash (pumpkins and marrows). They all grew quickly in hot American summers, and could be dried and stored for winter use.

How did early Americans carry heavy loads?

In South America, people carried loads using a cloth sling

which went across their foreheads and over their shoulders. In North America, people used dogs to haul a triangular sledge made of wooden poles, called a "travois". There were no horses in America until later times. The peoples of Central America did know how to make wheels, but did not use them for transport. The mountain paths they travelled were too steep and narrow for wheeled vehicles.

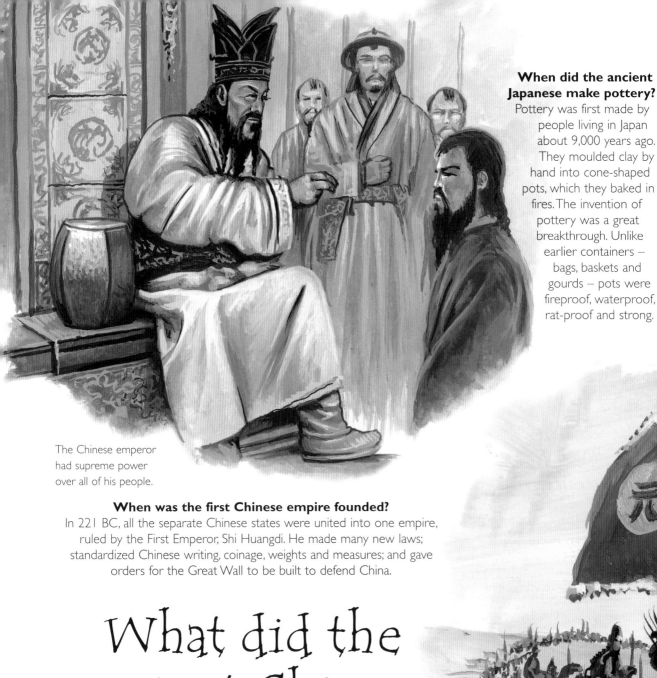

The Chinese emperor had supreme power over all of his people.

When did the ancient Japanese make pottery?
Pottery was first made by people living in Japan about 9,000 years ago. They moulded clay by hand into cone-shaped pots, which they baked in fires. The invention of pottery was a great breakthrough. Unlike earlier containers – bags, baskets and gourds – pots were fireproof, waterproof, rat-proof and strong.

When was the first Chinese empire founded?
In 221 BC, all the separate Chinese states were united into one empire, ruled by the First Emperor, Shi Huangdi. He made many new laws; standardized Chinese writing, coinage, weights and measures; and gave orders for the Great Wall to be built to defend China.

What did the ancient Chinese invent?

THE ANCIENT CHINESE WERE AMONG THE WORLD'S GREATEST INVENTORS.
Proper paper was first made by royal official Cai Lun around AD 105. We do not know who invented wood-block printing, but it was first used in China around AD 800. Chinese scientists had discovered how to make gunpowder about 100 years earlier. They soon found it could be used to create beautiful fireworks – as well as bombs and land-mines. Chinese inventors also made the first kites and umbrellas.

Who set sail across the Pacific?

Thousands of years ago, people from south-east Asia loaded their families, animals, farm tools and vegetable seeds in wooden canoes, and went in search of new land. Over the centuries, they founded settlements on many Pacific islands.

When did the first settlers reach Australia?

Nobody knows for certain, but it was probably 50,000 years ago, and maybe much earlier. Archaeologists think people arrived in Australia by sea from the Asian mainland. Once there, they quickly found ways of surviving in the vast land's harsh environment.

Which warrior stopped fighting to pray for peace?

Indian king Ashoka, who ruled from around 272 to 232 BC, was a famous warrior. But after the Battle of Kalinga, where 100,000 soldiers were killed, he began to hate violence. He decided to follow the Buddhist religion, and made many new laws to bring about peace.

Where was the Great Bath?

IT WAS IN MOHENJO-DARO, AN ANCIENT CITY IN THE INDUS VALLEY (NOW PART of Pakistan). From around 2600 to 1700 BC, people there worked as farmers, traders, artists and craft workers, under the rule of powerful "priest-kings". They built huge cities with comfortable homes, drains and running water. Each city had an open-air bath. The Great Bath was probably used for ritual washing, to purify priests before religious ceremonies.

What was the Silk Road?

It was a network of paths running 7,000 km (4,350 mi) across Asia, linking China to Europe and the Middle East. It was used by merchants travelling to buy silk and porcelain from China. The most famous journey along the Silk Road was made by Venetian adventurer Marco Polo (AD 1254–1324).

Traders travelled the Silk Road in "caravans" where camels and horses carried the traders in long lines across the desert.

Index